SHY GUIDES

GETTING OUT AND GETTING ALONG

The Shy Guide to Making Friends and Building Relationships

by Karen Latchana Kenney

Consultant:
Christopher A. Flessner, Ph.D.
Associate Professor, Department of Psychological Sciences
Director, Pediatric Anxiety Research Clinic (PARC)
Kent State University
Kent, Ohio

COMPASS POINT BOOKS
a capstone imprint

Compass Point Books are published by Capstone
1710 Roe Crest Drive, North Mankato, Minnesota 56003
www.mycapstone.com

Library of Congress Cataloging-in-Publication Data
Names: Kenney, Karen Latchana, author.
Title: Getting out and getting along : the shy guide to
  making friends and building relationships / by Karen
  Latchana Kenney.
Description: North Mankato, Minnesota : Compass
  Point Books, [2019] | Series: Shy guides | Includes
  bibliographical references and index.
Identifiers: LCCN 2018045895| ISBN 9780756560188
  (library binding) | ISBN 9780756560225 (pbk.) | ISBN
  9780756560263 (ebook pdf)
Subjects: LCSH: Bashfulness in children—Juvenile
  literature. | Interpersonal relations in children—
  Juvenile literature. | Friendship in children—Juvenile
  literature.
Classification: LCC BF575.B3 K46 2019 | DDC 155.42/3—
  dc23
LC record available at https://lccn.loc.gov/2018045895

Editorial Credits
Abby Colich, editor; Kay Fraser, designer;
Morgan Walters, media researcher; Laura Manthe,
production specialist

Image Credits
Shutterstock: Asia Images Group, 41, Cookie Studio, 17,
CREATISTA, 37, Daisy Daisy, 42, Daniel M Ernst, 26, 31,
Dean Drobot, 6, Diana Grytsku, 43, Elena Elisseeva, 34,
Featureflash Photo Agency, bottom 15, Flamingo Images,
11, gpointstudio, 33, Iakov Filimonov, 18, 23, Imagincy, 20,
Just2shutter, 16, Leonard Zhukovsky, bottom 9, LightField
Studios, 24, Mettus, Cover, 1, Monkey Business Images,
5, 13, 19, pixelheadphoto digitalskillet, 45, PrinceOfLove,
top 9, Rawpixel.com, 3, 7, 27, 28, s_bukley, bottom 21,
Samuel Borges Photography, top 21, wavebreakmedia, 38,
WindNight, top 15

Printed in the United States of America.
PA49

TABLE OF CONTENTS

CHAPTER 1

UNDERSTANDING QUIET

>>>>>>>>

You get to a party at your classmate's house, but your good friend isn't there yet. You only recognize a few faces. You see people you've met a few times and others who are complete strangers. You're not quite sure where to stand or who to talk to. You start getting hot and fidgety. What do you do?

The idea of going to a party can make some people uncomfortable, especially if there will only be a few people they know there. Some people may get nervous when meeting new people and making new friends. They don't know what to say or how to act. It's a feeling that a lot of people know well.

Do you ever feel this way? Maybe you're afraid that others might not like you. Do you think you'll say or do the wrong thing? Maybe you simply feel drained when you're in places with a lot going on. Those feelings can keep you from talking to others or spending a lot of time in social situations. If you feel this way, it's OK. It happens to a lot of people. But that doesn't mean you can't go out and make new friends. There's a wonderful friend inside you who wants to connect with others. You don't need to be the loudest, funniest person to feel good in social situations. You just need to find the ways of socializing that work for you.

WHY ARE YOU QUIET?

Everyone is quiet for different reasons. It can be helpful to understand the different reasons that make people who they are.

You may be shy or introverted. You also may be a little of both. If you are shy, you might be afraid of talking to other people. Introverted people feel drained if they are around others for too long. They shut down and need time alone before being social again. Don't worry too much about why you are quiet. Focus on accepting who you are and understand that you don't need to change to be a great friend to others.

Social Anxiety

Some people have social anxiety. Social anxiety is an extreme fear of social situations. This fear may cause people to avoid going to parties or other events. If you think you have anxiety or another mental health disorder that affects your everyday life, ask for help. Tell a trusted adult. An adult can help connect you with a counselor or doctor. Page 46 also has resources that can help you.

>>>>>> QUIZ: WHAT'S YOUR PERSONALITY?

Take this quiz to find out more about who you are. Answer yes or no to each question.

1. Do you like hanging out with a few friends better than a large group?

2. Are you a great listener?

3. Do you take the time to think before you speak?

4. After hanging out with your friends for a while, do you start to feel tired or drained?

5. Do you feel tense and stiff around people you don't know very well?

6. Do you sometimes have trouble thinking of things to say?

If you mostly answered "yes," you're likely a more shy or introverted person. Being around other people may drain you of energy. If you answered "no" to most of the questions, you're more likely an extrovert. Being alone can be difficult for you. You get more energy being in social situations. Both personality types have lots of positive traits. Try to focus on your positive traits as you discover more about who you are and how you can thrive in social situations.

CHAPTER 2

FROM ALONE TIME
TO FRIEND TIME

What's your idea of the perfect afternoon? Does it involve a book and a beanbag? Perhaps you like playing video games during your free time. Or maybe you like taking long bike rides. A lot of people value alone time. Being alone helps you relax and rest. Alone time might give you energy to go out and be social later. But if you spend too much time alone, you might start to feel lonely. Loving alone time doesn't mean that you don't want friends. You just need to balance it with some friend time too.

Everyone can make friends. Friends are important to have. They are the people you can say anything to. You can tell them your funniest jokes or act goofy with them without feeling dumb. They're there for fun adventures and even when you're sad. You can rely on them, and they make life more exciting.

We all have different kinds of friends. Some friends are more like acquaintances. You know them, but not really well. Close friends are people you know well. You have built a strong relationship with them. Close friends might start out as acquaintances. But as you get to know them better, they can become your best friends. Some friends stay acquaintances, and that's OK. It doesn't matter how many friends or acquaintances you have. Knowing yourself and your likes will help you choose friends who are right for you.

>> Kevin Durant

In an interview after winning the 2018 NBA finals, Golden State Warriors star Kevin Durant called himself an introvert. But this has never held him back in sports. He gave credit to his coach and teammates for their part in having a successful basketball season. He says his coach told him not to worry about what other people say. His team embraced him for who he is and didn't try to change him. They wanted him to be himself.

Maybe you're not the kind of person who can walk into a group and join in on the conversation right away. That's OK. You don't have to be that kind of person to make friends. We all make friends in different ways.

It helps to first know yourself and your strengths. You'll figure out all the wonderful qualities you have to offer a friend. Ask people you know what they like about you or what they think you are good at. See if they can come up with at least three things. Enlist family members or a friend. It may surprise you what they say. What comes easily to you may be difficult for others. Pay attention and really listen. Sometimes it takes someone else's observations to help you understand yourself better.

Then look at your own observations about yourself. Think about what you really like to do and what you're really good at, and be honest. If you like building robots or learning obscure facts about bugs—own it. Your interests make you who you are. Be proud of who you are, even if some of your interests aren't popular. Having confidence about what you like will attract other people. They'll want to know more about you.

LIFE TIP

Brainstorm a list of your interests and strengths. What are your favorite books, movies, and music? Write down what you're really good at and the things you care about, such as animals, soccer, or painting.

>>>>> Know Your Strengths

You may have many strengths that others might not realize right away.
Many quiet people are great at:

- listening carefully to others

- paying attention to details

- solving problems

- being loyal and caring friends

- motivating themselves to do things

- being creative

STARTING SMALL: FRIENDSHIP GOALS

Once you know more about who you are, you'll have a better idea about what you can offer a friend. But the goal of making new friends can still seem impossibly big. Where do you start?

Like with any big goal, you need to take small steps to get there. Friendships start small, but they need to start *somewhere*. Being friendly is one of the first keys to meeting someone new. Start with some simple goals:

- ☐ Say "hello" to someone in the hallway at school.

- ☐ Ask someone you don't know to be your partner for a class project.

- ☐ Talk to someone who is usually sitting alone at lunch.

- ☐ Offer to assist someone who looks like he or she needs help.

Try a new goal each day or week. You can even write down a list of goals. Cross them off as you accomplish them. On your first try, it might seem scary. But facing your fears will help you overcome them. Each goal will get a little easier the second or third try. Be patient with yourself. You're not going to be a pro right away, but you'll see these small goals adding up over time. You'll start meeting some new people. Meeting people is the first step in making new friends.

CHAPTER 3

>>>>>>>>>>>

YOU ARE NOW LEAVING YOUR COMFORT ZONE

Do you sit in the same spot in the lunchroom every day, next to the same people? Do you have an after-school routine that never changes—straight home for homework, snack, and then reading? If you do the same things every day, you may be stuck in your comfort zone.

Your comfort zone is all the habits and actions you do every day that you've gotten used to. These habits and actions make you feel safe and comfortable. You know what to do and what to expect. It's perfectly normal to have a comfort zone—everyone has a comfort zone. But it's important to get out of it too.

Don't let your comfort zone limit what you do. Challenge yourself to try new things. Trying new things will help you grow as a person. With every new situation you are in, there will be new people to meet. That means more opportunities to make new friends.

LIFE TIP

Keep a journal of the things you do every day. Just make a short list. You'll start to see your patterns, and you might be surprised by what they are. But knowing them will help you change them.

>>>> Zendaya

Actress Zendaya is best known for her roles in *Shake It Up*, *The Greatest Showman*, and two *Spider-Man* movies. As a child, she was very shy. She even had to repeat kindergarten because of her shyness. Even though she didn't want to, Zendaya's parents encouraged her to try performing. Once she was on stage, she loved it. All it took was for her to try something new one time.

MAKE THE CHANGE

Are you ready to leave your comfort zone? And where are you going? Take action to find new opportunities. Sign up for a class or a club at school that you wouldn't normally choose. In fact, pick something that's the opposite of what you always do. Try karate, chess club, or band. You may love it, and even if you don't, at least you'll have tried something new. If you do love an activity, you'll meet other people with a similar interest. That connection can help spark a friendship.

At first, try changing just one thing in your everyday routine. At lunch, sit at a different table. Talk with someone new. Ask someone in your class to hang out after school. Smile at someone you don't know.

As you become more confident outside of your comfort zone, try some more challenging activities. Host a small party. Invite some of the new people you've met. Keep it short and fun. Plan games you can play together. Your guests will all get to know one another a little better. You can also try joining some groups or classes that push you more into the spotlight, such as a debate club or an acting class. With each step, you'll learn more about yourself and meet other people who like to do the same things as you.

>>> 3 Ways to Break Out of the Zone

Try these ideas to get out of your comfort zone and connect with others.

1. Sign up for a pottery, photography, painting, or other kind of artistic class. You'll express yourself and meet others interested in art too.

2. Find a book club. Book clubs bring together the quiet activity of reading in a social group setting. Pick a group that reads the kinds of books you like.

3. Raise your hand to answer some of your teacher's questions. If you know what the class is discussing that day, write down some thoughts before you go. It helps to have notes to look at. Your classmates will get to hear your thoughts and may learn more about you.

FIRST IMPRESSIONS

You're at the first meeting of a new group or club you joined. You see a lot of new faces. Maybe you're really nervous. You might not talk to anyone or smile. Maybe you're sitting alone. Inside, your heart is beating fast and you feel really hot. But on the outside, people might think you're not interested in making friends. They get an impression of you, based on how you act and look. When you try something new and meet a new person, you're making a first impression. This is how people first see you when they meet you.

Now imagine that you smiled at someone or just said hello. You'd seem a lot friendlier. You don't have to change *who* you are to make that good first impression. You just need to be aware of how you look to others. You can make some small changes, like simply smiling, to look more open to meeting people.

LIFE TIP

Here are a few tips to make a good first impression:

- Smile and say hello.

- Make eye contact.

- Stand up tall. Don't slouch or slump over.

- Be kind and polite.

CHAPTER 4
SMALL TALK
AND BEYOND

>>>>>>>>>

After you've made your first impression, what comes next? Try some small talk. Small talk is a more casual way of talking. Simple questions that are easy to answer, like, "How are you today?" and "How is the weather?" are examples of small talk. To some people it can seem pointless and have little meaning. Small talk is important, though. It breaks the ice and makes a connection with others. It's great for speaking with acquaintances. Small talk can open the door to deeper conversations. It makes you seem friendly too. The right small talk can make a great first impression.

LIFE TIP

Is there someone else you notice who is quiet too? His or her personality might be like yours. But don't rule out the louder people. They may have qualities that are really different from yours, but also fit well with your personality.

>> Robert Pattinson

Robert Pattinson rose to fame starring as Edward Cullen in the *Twilight* saga. Though today he may be comfortable in front of the camera, he has hasn't always been the most social, especially as a teen. "I was shy, withdrawn and I didn't have any self-esteem," he said. "The year that I was 17 was one of the worst of my life, because I was searching for my place." He still doesn't like to give interviews. He says he prefers "to do things where I have a little time to think about what I'm saying first."

SMALL-TALK STARTERS

How do you start the small talk? First, you should be curious and interested in learning about others. What does the person you want to talk with seem to be interested in? Is she always reading comic books? Is he a math whiz? Does she like to draw cats on pretty much *everything*? Pay attention and notice what the person likes before you start a conversation.

Start chatting by asking a question such as, "How did you figure out that fraction so fast?" Or give a compliment such as, "Nice comic book!" It shows you are interested in knowing more about that person.

Try to keep the small talk going. Listen to the person's answers. Make good eye contact while you're listening too. It shows you are paying attention. Add your thoughts and think of follow-up questions from that person's answers. You may find that you really have something in common. If you do, talk about it. And guess what? You just took a step from small talk into a deeper conversation!

Like most things, small talk takes some practice to master. It might seem awkward at first, but each attempt teaches you what works and what doesn't. If you're nervous, break it down. Ask yourself, *What's the worst thing that can happen?* You may not hit it off with one person, but there are plenty of other people you will connect with. After you try some small talk, think about what worked and what didn't. Build on what works and try again with someone new. Over time, you'll develop your own small-talk style.

>>> Your Go-To Glossary of Small-Talk Phrases

It may help to have some small-talk phrases on hand. If you are nervous and can't think of something to say, you can use one of them. Here are a few to try:

- *What did you do this weekend?* This is an open-ended question. It needs more than a "yes" or "no" answer. It'll likely get someone chatting.

- *What's your favorite part in that book?* This connects with someone's interest—books, movies, and more. They will be more likely to chat about something if they enjoy it.

- *Nice sweatshirt! So did you like music camp?* Notice a music camp logo on someone's sweatshirt? Give her a compliment about it. It makes her feel good. And it opens the door for more chitchat. She's wearing it for a reason. It says something about who she is.

- *Did you see the end of the game last night?* Do you like a certain sports team and know someone else does too? Or was there a game your whole town is talking about? Sports are a great way to start a conversation.

CONVERSATION KILLERS

Sometimes a conversation hits a patch of dead silence...just crickets. It's awkward. It's quiet. What just happened?

You may have accidentally killed the conversation. Don't worry though, it happens to everyone. Did you just describe every detail about a wart on your foot? Or did you just say your friend looked really, really tired? Saying personal things like that can cut small talk short. Keep the conversation light if you can. It's probably best to save the personal stuff for deeper conversations with close friends.

Or maybe that silence has nothing to do with you at all. Your friend could be distracted or having a bad day. For example, your friend might seem super antsy and keep looking at the time. He might have to be somewhere in five minutes but doesn't want to seem rude.

If you don't want the conversation to be over, try one of your go-to small-talk phrases. It might spark the conversation to continue. But don't push it. Pay attention to what your friend says and does. If it seems like he wants to get going or if you do, exit the conversation politely. You might say, "I need to get going." Or, "It was great seeing you!" Both work great. You can even add something about the next time you meet, like "See you in class!" It ends the conversation on a positive note.

TALKING
IN GROUPS

Small talk is a great way to start a one-on-one conversation. But what if there's a group of people talking after school or soccer practice? You can use small talk to join in on a group discussion.

Don't be afraid of large groups. Yes, they can be loud. The topic may change quickly. It may seem like one person is doing all the talking. Knowing when to talk and how to be heard can be hard, but it is possible.

First, know that you're probably not going to be talking about something very deep. The conversation will likely be about a new TV show, a video game, or some funny thing that happened that day. Pay attention to what other people are talking about. Then see if it's something you're interested in too.

If you're nervous, start with small phrases. Add little comments to show that you agree or understand. "Yeah, totally!" or "You're kidding!" or even "You're right!" Even a smile, chuckle, *um-hmmm*, or nod adds to the conversation. It shows you're really listening and understanding what the other people are talking about.

If you have something to say, wait until there is a pause in the conversation. Make sure you speak in a voice that's loud enough to be heard. If you're too quiet, no one will be able to hear you. If you are interrupted, don't take it personally. It's just part of talking in a group.

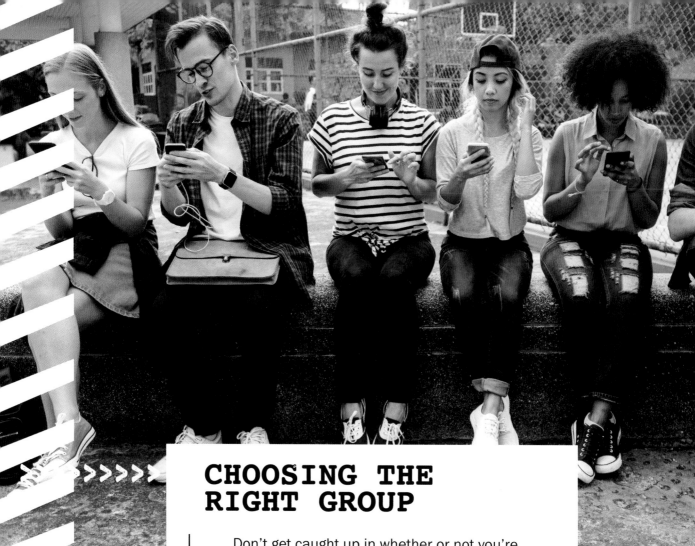

CHOOSING THE RIGHT GROUP

Don't get caught up in whether or not you're joining the most popular group. Popularity isn't as important as it may seem. Not all people will be in the most popular groups. Look at everyone in your school as being possible friends—popular or not. Be inclusive, not exclusive.

Sometimes the group conversations, whether with popular people or not, can turn negative. People may gossip or complain. If this happens, don't add to the negativity. Try to turn the conversation more positive to lighten it up. Try changing the subject. Ask if anyone else is nervous about the upcoming math test. Or ask everyone what their plans are for the weekend.

Real friendships are based on common values and respect for each other. They're the kind that last. Some groups of friends could break up at any moment. Friendship based on bullying, gossip, or other negativity and bad behavior shouldn't have a place in your life. It's a fake kind of friendship that won't last. Keeping the conversations positive and constructive with your friends will help make your relationships healthy and strong.

>>>> What Social Media Doesn't Tell You

Social media can be a great way to connect with others. However, don't forget what others post isn't always real. Selfies in perfect lighting and posts showing people having fun don't always show the whole picture. Most people don't post pictures of themselves feeling lonely, having a bad day, or doing unexciting things. Some users create an image of their lives in which everything looks great and exciting. Remember that and take some social media breaks. It will clear your head from the constant feeds.

FINDING YOUR CHARISMA

Once you've got the basics of individual and group conversation down, try adding to those. One way to do this is to find your charisma. Ever notice how some people seem to easily attract friends? Others feel good around them and just want to be near them. Having charisma means you show that you care about others. It doesn't mean you're overly excited about everything. That can seem fake and forced. Instead, let your own kind of charisma shine through.

So how do you develop charisma? First, really be *there* when you're talking to someone. Don't think about how much homework you have to do or where you need to be in an hour. Try not to fidget or look around. Just focus on your friend, right in that moment. Nod to show you're listening.

Then balance your interest in others with confidence in yourself. Show that you are relaxed and comfortable when conversing with others. If you're not sure what someone else is talking about, ask follow-up questions so that you understand better.

Focus on the positive too. You have a choice about how you think about every situation. Choose to be more positive in your thinking. Then share that positive attitude with others. Make positive comments to the people you talk with. They'll feel good about you and themselves after your conversation.

>>> Body Talk

Charisma and the words you use are important, but they're not everything. Your body communicates too. The expression on your face, how you stand, where you look—these are your actions. And they can speak loudly enough to be heard. During conversations, put your phone away. This will let you focus on the person you're talking with. Make eye contact occasionally, but don't stare. Uncross your arms. Crossed arms can communicate that you are closed off. Instead, put your hands in your pockets. Watch other people have conversations. Notice what they do. Then be aware of how you hold your body. You can adjust how you move to communicate that you care.

CHAPTER 5

MAKING AND KEEPING FRIENDS

>>>>>>>

Keep practicing your new conversation skills. Those conversations will likely lead to some new acquaintances. And that's great—it's good to be friendly with the people you see every day. But a friend is someone you feel completely comfortable with. And that's a special thing.

Turning an acquaintance into a friend takes time. A friendship develops in stages. It doesn't just happen overnight. Building a friendship is work, but it is also fun. As you get to know someone better, you let that person into your life. This means opening up—telling your friend some personal things. These things include problems, goals, and feelings. It's part of getting to know someone well. It shows that you trust that person to keep your secrets.

Opening up to someone can make you feel vulnerable. This can be a little scary at first. You don't know how others will react. But it is an important part of turning an acquaintance into a friend. Ease into opening up by starting small. Just say something kind of personal and see how that person reacts. Talk about a class assignment that is frustrating you or an upcoming sports game you're nervous about. Does your friend seem supportive? Does he tell you something personal too? If that person opens up too, it shows he wants to be a closer friend.

EMPATHY MATTERS

Another part of being a good friend is understanding and considering what others are feeling. This is called empathy. It guides how you act and what you say. An empathetic friend won't just think of himself. He'll consider his friend's feelings before talking. Imagine that your friend's pet guinea pig just died. You probably wouldn't want to tell him all about your new pet snake. It might make him miss his pet and feel sad.

How do you guess someone else's feelings if you don't know what's wrong? Look at her body language. Listen to what she's saying. Do you get the sense that something's wrong? Do you just feel it? That's your intuition. Listen to it. It means you know something's up.

Show your friend that you care. Ask her if everything is OK. She may not want to talk about it or she might share what's going on. Either way, she'll know that you care about her.

LIFE TIP

It's easy to get mad if you think someone is being mean or rude to you. But before you do, practice empathy. You don't know what's happening in that person's life. Try to think of that person's perspective before you act.

>>>> DO YOU HAVE EMPATHY?

Take this quiz to see how much empathy you have.

1. Your friend is upset she didn't make the cheerleading squad. Seeing her that way makes you feel:
   a) angry
   b) happy
   c) sad
   d) bored

2. It upsets you when people at school make fun of someone's haircut.
   a) never
   b) sometimes
   c) always
   d) rarely

3. When my friends talk to me about their problems, I:
   a) try to change the subject.
   b) stare off into the distance and tune them out.
   c) listen closely, look them in the eyes, and ask questions.
   d) start looking at my phone.

4. Pick the answer that's most like you.
   a) I like making people feel annoyed.
   b) I get annoyed when people are having fun.
   c) I like making people feel happy.
   d) I am too busy to worry about other people's feelings.

If you answered all C's, you have a lot of empathy for others. If you chose a few C's, or none at all, try to think of some ways you can be more empathetic. If someone talks to you about a problem, imagine what it's like to be that person. Think about the emotions he or she is experiencing. Like most things, learning to have empathy takes time. Try to remind yourself to be more empathetic each time you talk to someone. Slowly, your ability to be empathetic will improve.

CHAPTER 6

FRIENDSHIP BREAKS
AND BREAKUPS

>>>>>>>>

Sometimes you want to hang out with a friend every day. You have the best time together. But then you have a fight and you're not getting along. Sound familiar? Even if you love your best friend, you're going to have fights and disagree from time to time. Every relationship you have in life will go through ups and downs. Things can't be perfect every day. Dealing with the ups is easy, but what about the downs? How do you deal with them without harming your friendship?

Remember what made you friends in the first place. That is the core of your friendship. And if you have a good core, then the day-to-day issues that come up likely won't shake that core. Whether your friend broke some plans to meet up or hasn't returned your text in a few days, remember that solid core. Try not to assume reasons for the problems until you get some facts. It's easy to imagine a bad explanation for your friend's absence, but you don't know what's happening. Give your friend a chance to explain before you cross her off your friend list. Your friendship is worth more than that.

>>>> TIME FOR YOURSELF

One way to deal with disagreements with friends is to prevent them before they even start. A key to a healthy you and healthy friendships is to make sure you're getting enough time for yourself.

You may not feel like being around other people 24/7. You could be a deep thinker who gets lost in your thoughts. You probably need some downtime, away from the busy activity of school and hanging out with friends. But not everyone knows what's going on in your mind.

Imagine a friend asks you to come over after school one day, but you've had a busy week with after-school activities every day. You need a break and some quiet time at home to relax. So you tell your friend no. Your friend might think you don't *want* to hang out with her. While she couldn't be more wrong, she doesn't know the truth.

Don't assume your friend knows what's going on in your head. It's important to explain yourself. Let your friend know that you just need some time to recharge and that it has nothing to do with how you feel about her. That's part of opening up to your friend. If she takes it personally, then maybe she isn't the best kind of friend for you. If she accepts you and your honesty, then she's probably a keeper in the friend department.

SPACE: A FRIENDSHIP'S BEST FRIEND

As much as you may need alone time, don't forget sometimes your friends will need their space also. Space from each other can also be a good thing. This can especially be true if you've had an argument or disagreement. Or maybe you've been spending too much time together. And even if you're best friends, you can get sick of each other. Your friendship can become clingy and needy. What you need is balance—time together *and* time apart. Having that time apart teaches you what you miss and like about being with another person. It can be hard to spend time apart, but it's a good thing for any friendship.

You friend might have things he wants or needs to figure things out on his own. Respect his needs, even if you really want to talk with him. Check in with him to see if he's OK, but don't text, call, or e-mail any more until he's ready. You don't want to bug your friend too much. There may also be things he's dealing with that you don't know about.

Your friend will appreciate the space you give him. It shows you have trust in your friendship. That trust means that you know your friend will get in touch with you when he's ready. When that time comes, have a chat about what happened. Be open and caring and listen to what he has to say.

LIFE TIP

Some fights have nothing to do with you. Your friend could be upset about something else in her life and she doesn't know what to do with those feelings. Sometimes negative feelings can come out when dealing with the people we care about the most, even if they don't deserve them. If this happens to you, it can be hard to be patient and understanding, but it's important to try.

TO FIX OR TO SAY GOODBYE

What if space from a friend isn't just a short-term break? What if it leads to the end of the friendship? It's something everyone experiences at least once in a lifetime. Some friendships just won't last. People change over time. Sometimes that means growing apart. Maybe you start to like different things and you just have less in common than you once did.

Friendships can end in a big fight, but many times it happens less dramatically. One of you stops calling or texting as often as you used to. Your friend always has reasons why she can't hang out. Or you're both not as excited to see each other when you do meet.

If you're not ready to give up on a friendship, try talking about it first. Ask your friend if she's mad at you about something and if she wants to talk about it. Ask gently. Don't make your friend feel like you're accusing her of something.

Maybe your friend took something you said the wrong way. A simple apology can go a long way. Forgive each other and move on. And if you just can't agree on something, learn to compromise. Try to find ways to meet in the middle.

Talking about a problem may fix the friendship, but maybe it won't. If your friendship is over, it will hurt for a while. But don't get angry and hostile. Remember what brought you together as friends. Hold onto that memory. Try to figure out what you can learn from the experience. Then take what you've learned into future friendships. It may make you into a better friend.

GET OUT AND BE FRIENDLY

Everyone needs friends. Friendships start by getting out of your comfort zone and into the world. You'll meet lots of people once you start trying new things. Some of the people you meet will become good acquaintances. Others will become good friends that can last your entire life. Be open and start talking, and trust that some people will "get" you and want to start a friendship. From there, and with a little work, your friendship will grow.

Having a good friend is worth the work and care it takes to keep a friendship going and growing. Just remember to stay true to who you are and you'll attract friends who like the "real" you. It may take some time, but be patient and believe in yourself. True friends are worth the wait!

ASK FOR HELP

If you believe you're suffering from anxiety, depression, or another mental health issue or are the victim of bullying, ask for help. Reach out to a teacher, school counselor, parent, or another trusted adult. Doctors, psychologists, and social workers are available to get you the help you need. You can also reach out to one of these organizations below.

National Safe Place
provides immediate help and safety to any youth in crisis
https://www.nationalsafeplace.org/
Text SAFE and your current location to 4HELP (44357) for immediate help.

National Suicide Prevention
Lifeline national network of local crisis centers that provide free and confidential
    support
https://suicidepreventionlifeline.org/
800-273-8255

Stomp Out Bullying!
national nonprofit dedicated to preventing bullying, cyberbullying, and other
    digital abuse
http://stompoutbullying.org/

Teen Line
teen-to-teen hotline for when you just need someone to talk to
https://teenlineonline.org/
310-855-4673
Text TEEN to 839863.

Trevor Project
leading national organization providing crisis intervention and suicide prevention
    services to LGBTQ youth
https://www.thetrevorproject.org
866-488-7386
Text START to 678678.

READ MORE

Cain, Susan. *Quiet Power: The Secret Strengths of Introverts.* New York: Dial Books for Young Readers, 2016.

Criswell, Patti Kelley. *Friends: Making Them and Keeping Them.* Middleton, Wis.: American Girl, 2015.

Hemmen, Lucie. *The Teen Girl's Survival Guide: 10 Tips for Making Friends, Avoiding Drama and Coping with Social Stress.* Oakland, Calif.: Instant Help, an imprint of New Harbinger Publications, 2015.

INTERNET SITES

Use FactHound to find Internet sites related to this book.

Visit *www.facthound.com*

Just type in 9780756560188 and go.

 Check out projects, games and lots more at **www.capstonekids.com**

INDEX